Central England Verses
Edited by Claire Tupholme

YoungWriters

First published in Great Britain in 2007 by:
Young Writers
Remus House
Coltsfoot Drive
Peterborough
PE2 9JX
Telephone: 01733 890066
Website: www.youngwriters.co.uk

All Rights Reserved

© Copyright Contributors 2006

SB ISBN 1 84602 714 4

Foreword

Young Writers was established in 1991 and has been passionately devoted to the promotion of reading and writing in children and young adults ever since. The quest continues today. Young Writers remains as committed to the nurturing of poetic and literary talent as ever.

This year's Young Writers competition has proven as vibrant and dynamic as ever and we are delighted to present a showcase of the best poetry from across the UK and in some cases overseas. Each poem has been selected from a wealth of *A Pocketful Of Rhyme* entries before ultimately being published in this, our fourteenth primary school poetry series.

Once again, we have been supremely impressed by the overall quality of the entries we have received. The imagination, energy and creativity which has gone into each young writer's entry made choosing the poems a challenging and often difficult but ultimately hugely rewarding task - the general high standard of the work submitted ensured this opportunity to bring their poetry to a larger appreciative audience.

We sincerely hope you are pleased with this final collection and that you will enjoy *A Pocketful Of Rhyme Central England Verses* for many years to come.

Contents

Pedmore CE Primary School, Stourbridge

Owen Williams (9)	1
Harry Walton (9)	2
Charlotte Tiltman (9)	3
Olivia Thatcher (9)	4
Peter Stevens (9)	5
Megan Schlanker (10)	6
Alys Palfrey (9)	7
Phoebe Morris (9)	8
Hannah Morgan (9)	9
Adam Malik (9)	10
Niall Langford (9)	12
Jade Lane (9)	13
Alex Jones (9)	14
Charlie Hickman (9)	15
Elliot Harvey (9)	16
Ben Griffiths (9)	17
Joshua Follows (9)	18
Sam Field (9)	19
Eloise Farmer (9)	20
Meisam Faraji (9)	21
Chelsea Digby (9)	22
Georgina Cooper (9)	23
Anthony Collins (9)	24
Eleanor Bletcher (9)	25
Hannah Bayliss (10)	26
Kirsty Ackland (9)	27

St Chad's CE Primary School, Lichfield

Kimberley Waldron (10)	28
Emily Cannell (11)	29
Matthew Corry (10)	30
Chris Buckle (10)	31
Mia Greatrex (10)	32
Nicholas Stedman (10)	33
Katie Benham (10)	34
Danny Lee Sharp (10)	35

St George's CE (A) School, New Mills
Ben Bevan (10) — 36
Jack Henderson (10) — 37
Katie Cross (10) — 38
Rhys Jones (10) — 39

St John's CE Primary School, Ripley
Skye Cotes (9) — 40
Charlotte Penny (9) — 41
Suzanne Leo (10) — 42
Barbara Godkin (9) — 43
Emily Kate Potter (9) — 44
Ellie Morris (9) — 45

St Mark's CE (A) Primary School, Stoke-on-Trent
Zaynah Aslam (8) — 46
Ibraheem Rafeeq (8) — 47

St Mary Immaculate Catholic Primary School, Warwick
Nadine Griffin (10) — 48
Tiffany Wareing (9) — 49
Dana Harris (9) — 50
Blake Wareing (10) — 51
Ross Chamberlain (10) — 52
Sam Slemensek (10) — 53
Yasmin Feasey (10) — 54

St Mary's RC Primary School, Richmond
Aimee Duffy (10) — 55
Matthew Walker (10) — 56
Lee Sells (10) — 57
Richard Wade (10) — 58
Christopher Walker (10) — 59
Ross McGuigan (10) — 60
Joshua De Roche (11) — 61
Sophie Stewart (10) — 62
Thomas Moss (10) — 63
Rebecca Wenham (10) — 64
Hollie Pickersgill (10) — 65
Elizabeth McNamara (10) — 66

Blythe Mary Wright (10)	67
Rebecca Swift (10)	68
Dominic Wright (11)	69

St Wystan's School, Repton

George Gould (9)	70
Arun Gandhi (9)	71
Catherine Holden (9)	72
Eleanor Hodson Walker (9)	73
Holly Collins (9)	74
Tom Chandler (9)	75
Amber Holgate (9)	76
Stefan Harban (9)	77
Rebecca Downs (10)	78
Lucy Adams (9)	79

Thanet Primary School, Hull

Claire Louise Barr & Bethany Gray (9)	80
Connor Hadfield & Alex Foster (9)	81
Kieran Poskitt (9)	82
Aimey Freeman, Emily Attwood & Kelly Louise Phillipson (9)	83
Adam Kyle (9)	84
Connor Hemingway (9)	85
James Heath & Shane Radford (9)	86
Nathan Woolhouse & Lloyd Morrison (9)	87
Jordan Scott & Liam Alan Hutchinson (9)	88
Lauren Scarah & Amy Mail (9)	89
Adam Hilton (9)	90
Katie Drury (9)	91
Chloe Warrior (9)	92
Abbigail Clixby & Chloe Fothergill (9)	93
Ryan Thomas Weaver (9)	94
Lewis Taylor (9)	95

Warwick Junior School, Warwick

Seb Shields (9)	96
Sam Button (9)	97
James Cusworth (9)	98
Sam Martin (9)	99
Jai Hayer (9)	100

Willie Priestley (9)	101
Michael Richards (9)	102
Laurence Johnson (9)	103
Jamie Shillcock (9)	104
Alexander Harper (9)	105
Gordon Carr (9)	106
Joe Canning (9)	107
Callum James (9)	108
Alex Simpson (9)	109
Ollie Shearman (9)	110
Will Jackson (9)	111
Alex Fox (9)	112
Harnek Singh (9)	113
Louis Hawking (9)	114
Henry McGovern (9)	115
Toby Ashworth (9)	116
George Burbidge (9)	117
Tobias Sims (9)	118
Sam Hillcox (9)	119
Bhavan Thiara (9)	120
James Cleary (9)	121
Freddie Ashworth (9)	122
Sam Woodyatt (9)	123
Ben Taylor (9)	124
Richard Phillips (9)	125
Hamish Kerr (9)	126
Matthew Riley (9)	127
Tohmev Singh (9)	128
Harry Fitzpatrick (9)	129
Todd Freeman (10)	130

The Poems

Scared

Scared lives in a bare, deep, damp, smelly cellar
With rats crawling and mice squealing
There's a dull face with horrible scars
Sometimes he is petrified of bullies
Slamming his windows and cracking them
He wanders around the cellar with mischievous eyes
Sometimes his ears prick up as he listens to voices in the street
Scared thinks about his few friends and what they are doing
He wishes for some scraps of food
Or to win the lottery so he gets some money
He wants to work, but he is too scared.

Owen Williams (9)
Pedmore CE Primary School, Stourbridge

Fear

Fear hides in a dark old meadow, in a dull old cottage
His face is pale and white
He has ten gigantic scars
His daily food is fried rat and a cup of blood from one of his ten scars
He always talks to himself to try to calm himself down
He never goes to happy movies or programmes
He just scares himself at horror movies
Nobody knows why he scares himself, not even Fear himself knows
Fear hates his cottage, so he always goes outside
Grabs his rod, sits in the dirt putting bait on his rod
And starts waiting . . . just waiting
Nobody knows why he does it - there's nothing to catch
Then when he storms back into his dull old cottage he goes
                                                                up the stairs
Walks up to the very last room in the hall and crawls into bed
Sweating all on his own.

Harry Walton (9)
Pedmore CE Primary School, Stourbridge

Fear

Fear hides in a tumbledown shack
At the edge of a grey lake, by himself
Fear looks out at the world he is afraid of
Lighting his way, is one melted candle
And the dim cloud-covered winter sun
His friends are Misery, Darkness and Woe
His terrifying nemesis is everything happy
At night, he lies on a bed of nightmares
His black eyes are wide awake thinking of tomorrow -
Another day of fear.

Charlotte Tiltman (9)
Pedmore CE Primary School, Stourbridge

Friendly

Friendly is a smiling face
Eyes that shine with happiness
Always listening to secrets
Dancing through the daffodils
With yellow, wavy heads
Friendly is caring for everyone
Always ready to share.

Olivia Thatcher (9)
Pedmore CE Primary School, Stourbridge

Joyful

Joyful giggles when his friends tickle him
He has a smiley face with big blue eyes that sparkle
Joyful adores bouncing about!

Joyful's home is Aqualand, a water park in France
Joyful will always welcome you
He will let you go on the Black Hole -
A fantastic water slide in the dark!

Joyful's favourite food is pepperoni pizza - *mmm!*
He loves to drink bubbly lemonade.

Joyful's friends are Cheerful and Blissful and lots of others.

Peter Stevens (9)
Pedmore CE Primary School, Stourbridge

Nervous

Nervous lives in a dark place,
She hides whenever she can,
She always wears a hood,
Her hut is made of wood,
Her teeth are nearly always chattering,
Otherwise she's silent and still,
She's too scared to answer questions,
She always hides her face,
Her only friend is Cautious,
They both feel out of place.

Megan Schlanker (10)
Pedmore CE Primary School, Stourbridge

The Skate-Off

Ring! The bell goes and the music comes on
Winter comes out of the dressing room
Now it is astonishingly cold
Closely followed by spring
Who is still warm
Sausages
Burgers
Hot dogs
BBQ sauce
Doughnuts
Waffles
Chicken sticks.

Winter starts with a jump and a spin
The judges are impressed
She falls over and she twists her ankle
Denim shorts
Short-sleeved school shirts
Strappy T-shirts
Hat.

Spring comes out and does the one, the only
Triple spin with a double flip
Surfing
Bodyboarding
Building sandcastles
Scuba-diving
Water fights.

The judges give their marks
Winter has got a 5, 2, 1
Spring has got a 10, 10, 10!
Spring wins!
The crowd go wild, 'Fabulous! Fabulous!'
It's like a cold zoo in there
Let's hope Winter has not got the cold shoulder.

Alys Palfrey (9)
Pedmore CE Primary School, Stourbridge

Poorly

Poorly dwells in a graffitied hut
He rapidly lurks about, crying because he is poorly
Poorly is too frightened to leave his hut to get help
When it rains, water slowly drips from the roof of the hut.

The floor is damp, he has no toilet
Poorly has hundreds of diseases
His enemies are Happy, Joyful and Better
He has no friends.

His jaws chatter, like crab's pincers
He always twiddles his thumbs
With huge, black bags under his eyes.

Phoebe Morris (9)
Pedmore CE Primary School, Stourbridge

Shy

My feeling is shy
It hides in the cellar
Where spiders hide
It tiptoes because it's so scared
Oh no! There's a noise
It's terrified, it thinks it's its mom
Phew! She's gone
I think it would like to be lively from now on!

Hannah Morgan (9)
Pedmore CE Primary School, Stourbridge

The Match Of The Year

They're shaking hands and they're off!
Winter with the ball
What's this?
I have never seen this before
Autumn's midfielders are running for the ball
All they have to do is . . . yes! Goal!
Winter blasts the ball up field and before you know it . . .
It's a goal!
This is going to be one interesting match.

Leafless trees
Hibernating animals
Sparkling evergreens
Snow-covered pavements
Comforting fires
Vicious snowstorms.

They're close to the goal . . .
What a save from Winter's goalkeeper!
The strikers are close to the goal
Foul!
It's a free kick and it's a . . . goal!

All-out rough terrain
Snowball fights
Toboggan races
Swirling ice skaters
Top of the range snowboarding.

And their best player is on!
But he's lost the ball - I don't believe it
They've scored!
It's actually 3-1!

Steaming fudge cakes
Hot apple pies
A steaming mug of tea

Freshly made mince pies.

It's the last ten seconds
And Autumn's lagging . . .
It's a thunderous victory for Winter!

Adam Malik (9)
Pedmore CE Primary School, Stourbridge

Frightened

Frightened lives in an abandoned cottage
With bats that are clinging onto the thick, dark door
Frightened's friends don't come to the abandoned cottage
Spiders climb on his scruffy hair.

Niall Langford (9)
Pedmore CE Primary School, Stourbridge

Petrified

Petrified lives in the ruins of a tower,
Petrified has a horrified expression on his face,
He lies at night and drools all over his tatty, old clothes
And counts himself lucky.

Petrified's eyes are greyish-bagged,
He drools deeply,
Petrified was abandoned in a flowing river
And had brought himself up since.

Petrified doesn't know his name, age or date of birth,
Unlike us, Petrified is wild and doesn't go to school,
Petrified never sets foot outside of the tower,
Sometimes, Petrified hides when visitors come.

Jade Lane (9)
Pedmore CE Primary School, Stourbridge

Enjoyment

Enjoyment is the most amazing person in the universe
Being with them is the same as somebody lifting you up
                              when you're down
Enjoyment has its arms open for you all the time
He slowly travels around the world to keep everybody joyful.

Alex Jones (9)
Pedmore CE Primary School, Stourbridge

Happy

Happy has a smiling face
Excitedly dancing about
Pink 'Groovy Chick' around the walls
Presents hiding under my bed.

Charlie Hickman (9)
Pedmore CE Primary School, Stourbridge

Fear

Fear dwells in a deserted house
That has shattered windows and a hanging door
He hides in his crammed box, shivering
Fear dashes across, under the bed
With his little frightened eyes sticking out
Hooded, he leaps onto the bed, his face pale
Fear then grabs the bedsheets
And zooms downstairs like a petrified cheetah
His enemy is Angry, his face red-hot and a mean brain.

Elliot Harvey (9)
Pedmore CE Primary School, Stourbridge

Jealousy

Jealousy walked down his dim and foggy street
Having no friends and many enemies
His dark grey hair covers his dark grey face
And he lives in the top corner of a dimly lit flat
He won't come out, except on the blackest of nights
It rarely happens, so he has seen only darkness
No trees, no animal, nothing that lives
He will end his life friendless.

Ben Griffiths (9)
Pedmore CE Primary School, Stourbridge

Upset

Upset is old and small
And he lives in a cramped, ruined classroom
He wants nothing to do with anybody
He looks like a groaner
And has an upset life
Because nobody likes him.

Joshua Follows (9)
Pedmore CE Primary School, Stourbridge

Anger

Anger loves to inhabit an ancient dragon's cave
He's got fiery eyes and steam coming out of his ears
He's got black, spiky hair
Like an electrocuted person.

Anger rarely goes out
Because no one will be his friend
But deep down he knows that someone will be his friend.

Although he's angry, he's quite happy inside
Because he knows somewhere in the future
He'll have someone there.

Sam Field (9)
Pedmore CE Primary School, Stourbridge

Anger

Anger is steaming hot with a red face
And a devilish pair of eyes
He dwells in an old tatty cellar
With rats and mice
Even his friends are in fear of him
When he shouts, he nearly explodes!
He moves with his arms in front of him
Hunting for food.

Eloise Farmer (9)
Pedmore CE Primary School, Stourbridge

Terrified

In the dark, dark, silent night
Hiding in a small, old tate barrel
With rats crawling
And mice racing everywhere
And spiders creeping and crawling
He was there, frightened and panting
He almost bit his fingers off
He was shivering with fear.

Meisam Faraji (9)
Pedmore CE Primary School, Stourbridge

Deceitful

Deceitful lives in a hidden, miserable house
Crammed with unwanted furniture of sorts
Deceitful has a big mouth, happily chatting away
Everyone's most treasured secrets for the whole world to hear
Once trusted, now rejected, no friends, no family, no love
Just enemies that were once good friends
All he can do now is sob and wish
(Well he can only dream)
That he never started lying in the first place.

Chelsea Digby (9)
Pedmore CE Primary School, Stourbridge

Lonely

Lonely lurks deep down in a deserted subway
He eats nothing but stranded flies caught in webs and wood dust
Making boring, old, drowsy, unwanted objects like himself
He slowly walks further, hoping that one day he will approach
                                                    a bright white light
Which will take him to a new town, a new place
When he will be lonely no more.

Georgina Cooper (9)
Pedmore CE Primary School, Stourbridge

Heartbroken

Heartbroken has lost his family
Heartbroken deserted his house
Heartbroken lost a murder case
For ten long years
All alone
Because
Heartbroken has no friends
He has no place to live
Or family
Except for a hole with a gravestone.

Anthony Collins (9)
Pedmore CE Primary School, Stourbridge

Swim Of The Year!

The trophy has been put down
And the gun has just gone *bang!*
All the swimmers are in the water
And have started their strokes.

Leaves
Crunch
Colour
Ripe
Full
Floats.

Summer can't beat Autumn
Because Autumn has the *wow* factor!

Hail
Rain
Wind
Sun
Grey sky.

Autumn's in front
How will Autumn be beaten?

Dates
Figs
Apricots
Raisins
Harvest time.

The best month's swim has just ended
The trophy has just been lifted!

Big moons
Dark nights
Shadowy objects
Bright stars.

Eleanor Bletcher (9)
Pedmore CE Primary School, Stourbridge

Shy

Shy is funny
He walks on tiptoes
And speaks with a murmur.

Shy hides in an abandoned classroom
Under an ancient, rickety table
With empty walls and nothing but spiderwebs
Everywhere you go.

Shy has a problem:
He is petrified . . .
. . . Petrified of rats!

Shy will be sprinting soon
Sprinting away
To find somewhere to stay for the night.

I wonder what will happen to him?
Who knows?
Who knows?

Hannah Bayliss (10)
Pedmore CE Primary School, Stourbridge

The Arrow Of The Year

Summer has just pulled the string
And the arrow shoots off like it's red-hot
A bullseye!
There's no way Spring's going to gallop up the board now.

Sunny
Hot
Blue sky
Some shade.

Spring is still hopping around
On the bottom of the chart
Like a rabbit.

Ice cream
Strawberries
Oranges
Hot dogs.

Almost the end of the match
And Summer is scorching the board
With his shots.

Shorts
Caps
T-shirts
Sandals.

Spring can't fly
He's down
Summer is the winner!

Kirsty Ackland (9)
Pedmore CE Primary School, Stourbridge

Jealousy - A Fierce Tiger

Jealousy - a fierce tiger,
Clinging on to you,
Surprising, but unexpected,
Inside it creeps up on you,
Using huge paws, it catches you,
Making sure it doesn't let go.

Green with envy, waiting,
For its next unsuspecting victim,
Patiently waits,
Moving almost silently,
Stalking.

Sneaky, but clever,
It gets to you,
Lonely, furious, sly and unwanted,
Eating up your soul.

The angry eyes of jealousy,
Get to you,
You fall into its evil trap,
Jealousy is a fierce tiger.

Kimberley Waldron (10)
St Chad's CE Primary School, Lichfield

The Snow Fish

Snow, a colourful angelfish,
Scales like frosting snowflakes,
She swims solemnly down
Through the cool air.

Cold and dewy,
She moves with elegance,
Drifting down from the hazy sky,
She lies, dead, on the pallid rooftops.

Emily Cannell (11)
St Chad's CE Primary School, Lichfield

Hate!

Hate is a hungry T-rex,
As it boldly strides,
Its icy stare is dauntingly hard to kill,
It walks with a menacing stomp,
One colossal mouth blames another,
The deadly attitude is something to avoid,
Don't give in, because Hate is coming!

Matthew Corry (10)
St Chad's CE Primary School, Lichfield

The Thundering Tornado!

Thrashing tornado - a deadly, overgrown anaconda,
Slithering ear-piercingly through the eroded town,
Its deadly lashing terrorises the broken houses,
Laser eyes that shoot ice-cold blizzards from its rays,
Its murderous stare gilleting the destroyed country,
Rapidly tears the thundering, eerie sky,
The portal to death is coming for *you!*
Beware!

Chris Buckle (10)
St Chad's CE Primary School, Lichfield

Fog

White fog - a spooky ghost
Moving silently towards the lost houses
Making a moaning sound
Floating around the lonely town
It hugs the houses sadly
Feeling alone
And unwanted.

Mia Greatrex (10)
St Chad's CE Primary School, Lichfield

Angry Dragon

Anger is a furious, black dragon
Viciously tearing apart a helpless human
It roars a deafening sound
To make people run through the scary street
When it stomps out of its rocky cave
No one dares to go outside
Its dark red eyes could stop someone dead in their tracks
And make them wish they weren't there
And its impenetrable coat of diamonds
Could make a unit of cavalry stop and realise they couldn't win
Beware, Anger is deadly.

Nicholas Stedman (10)
St Chad's CE Primary School, Lichfield

Circling Snow

The snow - an angelfish swimming elegantly through the sky,
The scales were the magical sight of glacial snowflakes,
Moving with pure magnificence,
Active movements,
Circling the crystal sky calmly
And gently hitting the ground.

Katie Benham (10)
St Chad's CE Primary School, Lichfield

Anger Dragon

Anger is a furious red dragon
Roaring as it stomps out of its huge domain
Gliding over the land with its colossal wings
When it reaches a victim, it creeps behind them
Outraged from being awoken from its deep slumber
And strikes!

Danny Lee Sharp (10)
St Chad's CE Primary School, Lichfield

Teacher, Teacher

Teacher, teacher, what a disgrace
It's so mad, you can't face.

The kids, they are all running riot
Can't you tell them to *be quiet!*

Ben Bevan (10)
St George's CE (A) School, New Mills

Bikes, Bikes

Bikes, bikes, some are trikes more and more and more
Tyre marks on the floor doing the speed of a condor
Bikes, bikes, some are fat, some are thin
Try not to crash into a bin!
Crossers, road bikes, fast and slow
Ride them both in the snow!
Mechanic racers both wearing braces
Looking at their smiling faces
I put my thumb up and say, 'You're both aces!'

Jack Henderson (10)
St George's CE (A) School, New Mills

Grandma

My grandma is an angel,
High in the sky,
She became an angel,
In the month of July,
We love her so dearly,
It's a shame we had to part,
But she will always be with us,
Here in our hearts.

Katie Cross (10)
St George's CE (A) School, New Mills

Teachers Are Mean

Why are teachers really mean?
They are fat and really green
Their legs are hairy
They love their dairy
Why are teacher really mean?

They are fat and really green
I know a girl who knows a teacher
She said she's an ugly creature
Teachers are mean so stay away
They come out any day.

Rhys Jones (10)
St George's CE (A) School, New Mills

Autumn Time

The branches are people dancing in the breeze,
The fireworks are flowers in the sky,
The fire is a big, orange lion, roaring and roaring,
The brightly coloured leaves are dancing ladies in lovely dresses,
The howling wind is a monster on the prowl,
The night approaches, like a hunter running for a fox,
Children are ghosts and ghouls on Hallowe'en,
The nights are cold, like the North Pole,
Autumn is the best season ever!

Skye Cotes (9)
St John's CE Primary School, Ripley

Autumn

Trees calmly waving in the wind
Dancing wind round the roses
The wind is a swirling carousel
Different colours, red and orange and brown
Trees calmly dancing in the wind
The leaves are crunchy
Leaves falling off the trees
The leaves are swirling tornadoes
Sky darkening earlier in the day.

Charlotte Penny (9)
St John's CE Primary School, Ripley

Autumn Poem

The sky is a black ink pen,
The coloured leaves float around the sky like coloured pieces of paper,
The crunchy leaves are people eating crunchy bars,
The wind dances around the sky like ballerinas,
The trees are swaying dancers,
The leaves are hot air balloons flying around the street,
The trees sway in the blowing wind,
The leaves are beautiful coloured crisps,
The leaves are empty crisp packets blowing around the street,
Bang! Autumn ends!

Suzanne Leo (10)
St John's CE Primary School, Ripley

My Mum

My mum is a soft teddy bear,
My mum is a bright red robin in winter,
My mum is a bright yellow sunflower,
My mum is a lovely sunny day.

Barbara Godkin (9)
St John's CE Primary School, Ripley

My Mum

She's a silky dress,
She's a warm radiator,
She's a baby bear,
She's a soft breakfast orange,
She's a calm babysitter,
She's a bright, colourful sunset,
She's a bush of sweet lavender,
She's a light, glittering night.

Emily Kate Potter (9)
St John's CE Primary School, Ripley

Autumn Poem

The crunch of a twig is a crunchy cereal bar
The sky is turning to black coal
The leaves are whirlpools
Bonfire Night burnt leaves are dust
The leaves falling from the trees are biscuits;
Red, green, brown and orange
The leaves learning to dance are ballerinas
The children and adults are ghosts, ghouls and witches
Getting treats and scaring people
Fireworks *bang* and *boom* and are pretty flowers falling down.

Ellie Morris (9)
St John's CE Primary School, Ripley

A Day In The Life Of Rosy The Dog

Rosy wakes up
Eats
Runs out into the garden
She digs up her bone
And sleeps
Rosy wakes up
Eats
She comes in to eat her food
She finds a cosy place
And sleeps
Rosy wakes up
Goes into the garden
Chases her tail.

Zaynah Aslam (8)
St Mark's CE (A) Primary School, Stoke-on-Trent

A Day In The Life Of Ibraheem The Lion

Ibraheem wakes up
Eats
Finds meat
He returns
Has a race with Dan
And sleeps
Ibraheem wakes up
Eats
Breaks into the shed
Finds a cosy place
And sleeps
Ibraheem wakes up
Eats
Walks around the jungle
Looks for meat
Scratches himself
And sleeps
Ibraheem wakes up
Eats.

Ibraheem Rafeeq (8)
St Mark's CE (A) Primary School, Stoke-on-Trent

There Was An Old Lady From Kent

There was an old lady from Kent
Who wanted to live in a tent
Everyone really cried
When the old lady died
And all that was left was a dent.

Nadine Griffin (10)
St Mary Immaculate Catholic Primary School, Warwick

There Was A Young Lady From France

There was a young lady from France
Who really liked to dance
It happened when she tried
Her skirt flew off to her side
So she stood alone in her pants.

Tiffany Wareing (9)
St Mary Immaculate Catholic Primary School, Warwick

There Was A Small Cat Called Poppy

There was a small cat called Poppy
That was a little bit floppy
She saw a tiny dog
That chased a giant frog
Then Poppy went a bit soppy.

Dana Harris (9)
St Mary Immaculate Catholic Primary School, Warwick

There Was A Young Fellow Called Blake

There was a young fellow called Blake
That always ate a lot of cornflakes
They thought he was so small
But he was very tall
And he ate some delicious cake.

Blake Wareing (10)
St Mary Immaculate Catholic Primary School, Warwick

There Was An Old Man From Dundee

There was an old man from Dundee
Who always ate apples for tea
As he loved them a lot
He put them all in pots
And gave them to his friend called Lee.

Ross Chamberlain (10)
St Mary Immaculate Catholic Primary School, Warwick

There Was A Man With A Beard

There was a man with a beard
He found out he was very weird
He lost his red top hat
Under his stylish mat
And found he had disappeared.

Sam Slemensek (10)
St Mary Immaculate Catholic Primary School, Warwick

Spot

There was once a young dog called Spot
Who looked like a small tiny dot
He went to the seaside
To swim in the high tide
Then sailed away in a yacht.

Yasmin Feasey (10)
St Mary Immaculate Catholic Primary School, Warwick

Darkness

Darkness is black like the sky at night
It sounds like an owl in the tree at night
It tastes like the tea's gone cold.

Aimee Duffy (10)
St Mary's RC Primary School, Richmond

Anger

A nger is a scary sight
N early bites
G et ready because it's not like flying a kite
E rr, argh, anger hurts punching and kicking.
 You have to be mighty to fight anger
R un, hide, anger is near!

Matthew Walker (10)
St Mary's RC Primary School, Richmond

Happiness

Happiness is yellow like our sunny sun
It sounds like children having fun
It tastes like a lovely ice cream
It smells like a cheeseburger in a dream
It looks like a lot of children laughing
It feels like a wet dog after a bath
It reminds me of a nice warm feeling.

Lee Sells (10)
St Mary's RC Primary School, Richmond

Silence

Silence is as white as a cloud
It sounds like air flowing past your ears
Silence tastes like a scoop of ice cream
It smells like fresh air
It looks like a white cloud
It feels like a squidgy pillow
It reminds me of someone sneaking across the hall.

Richard Wade (10)
St Mary's RC Primary School, Richmond

Anger

Anger is the colour of a raging fire
Anger is the sound of people dying
Anger tastes like rotting animals
Anger smells like smoke in the air
Anger looks like an ugly troll
Anger feels like needles
Anger reminds me of pain.

Christopher Walker (10)
St Mary's RC Primary School, Richmond

Sadness

S adness can be upsetting
A t the sight of a broken heart
D ying of loneliness
N early rips your head apart
E ngagement is broken
S oaked by the crying tears
S aid to be forever, said that the end is near.

Ross McGuigan (10)
St Mary's RC Primary School, Richmond

Happiness

H earing the dog that has been found by its owner
A t that moment, everybody knew the owner was a loner
P eople with smiling faces all around
P eople singing with joy
I dentify their favourite, lovely toy
N o one knows how happy I am
E verybody gets me my favourite food and gives it to me
S o then I have to drink some rich tea
S o that's what happiness means to me.

Joshua De Roche (11)
St Mary's RC Primary School, Richmond

Darkness

D rumming sound in your head
A broken heart in pain
R emember the brightness calling out in vain
K now that it will never break
N ever beg for morning wake
E ven though it's so dark
S orrow won't call out the lark
S adness, darkness, sorrow and pain.

Sophie Stewart (10)
St Mary's RC Primary School, Richmond

Love

Love reminds me of strawberry ice cream
Love is pink like a flaming love arrow ready to attack
Love sounds like an angel singing
Love tastes like sweet sugar
Love smells like red roses
Love looks like people falling in love
Love feels like soft and cuddly toys.

Thomas Moss (10)
St Mary's RC Primary School, Richmond

Sadness

S ounds like the wail of a bear left on its own
A fter the loss of a loved one
D ying upsets relatives
N obody will see them until we meet in Heaven
E verybody who has heard, says nice things
S ad days will come again
S oon we will meet merrily in Heaven.

Rebecca Wenham (10)
St Mary's RC Primary School, Richmond

Happiness

Happiness is yellow like the sunshine on the first day of spring
I love it when the children sing
When my favourite food comes my way
I really don't know what to say
I'm happy when I'm with my friend
I always have something to lend
I'm happy when I watch TV
That's what happiness means to *me!*

Hollie Pickersgill (10)
St Mary's RC Primary School, Richmond

Love Is . . .

Love is pink like the cherry blossom on a tree
Love sounds like the angels' trumpets playing
Love tastes as sweet as sticky treacle and syrup
Love smells like perfume and flowers
Love looks like pink candyfloss shaped in love hearts
Love feels like soft, warm marshmallows in hot chocolate
Love reminds me of a fluffy, friendly dog!

Elizabeth McNamara (10)
St Mary's RC Primary School, Richmond

Sadness

S adness of a relation or neighbour who passes away
A nd how do you keep your emotions at bay
D own in the dumps is as far as you can go
N ever will you feel so low
E verybody will have a kind thing to say
S o listen out in every way
S adness will never stay, so be happy when you're having
a good day!

Blythe Mary Wright (10)
St Mary's RC Primary School, Richmond

Love

Love is pink, as happy as day
It sounds like the singing of angels away
It smells like a rose, red and beautiful
It looks like children with smiles on their faces
It feels like pillows made of feathers so soft
It reminds me of my godmother, the one that I lost.

Rebecca Swift (10)
St Mary's RC Primary School, Richmond

The Sea

The sea is as blue as the sky
The sea roars like a lion
The sea tastes like salt being thrown onto your salmon
The sea smells like a rose
The sea looks like a large scape of blue
The sea feels like a dream of happiness
The sea reminds me of you.

Dominic Wright (11)
St Mary's RC Primary School, Richmond

The Sea

Clear blue sky
Crying seagulls,
Large, puffy clouds
Glistening bright sun.

Sparkling clear sea
Roaring rough waves,
Children splashing
Smelly fishy odours.

Hot, sticky sand
Sharp, tall rocks,
Small, shiny rock pools
Children running and playing.

George Gould (9)
St Wystan's School, Repton

The Sea

The bright blue sky
Curvy seagulls
Rocky cliffs
White clouds.

Deep blue sea
Crab claws,
Lively ocean
Wonderful fish.

Sparkling sand
Deep rock pools,
Crabs running
Children playing.

Arun Gandhi (9)
St Wystan's School, Repton

The Sea

Sparkly blue sky,
Squawking seagulls.
Soft candyfloss clouds,
Smiling sunshine.

Sparkling seas,
Wonderful fish.
Fast, roaring waves,
Blue oceans.

Smooth sand,
Scattered pebbles.
Sandy hands,
Jagged rocks.

Catherine Holden (9)
St Wystan's School, Repton

The Sea

Blue clear sky
Squawking seagulls
Bright sparkling sun
Whispers of wind

Deep dark sea
Brightly coloured coral
Curved, smashing waves
Cold, foamy splashes

Gritty, hot sand
Children building sandcastles
Glistening rock pools
Smooth, shiny shells.

Eleanor Hodson Walker (9)
St Wystan's School, Repton

The Sea

The light blue sky,
With seagulls swooping,
Puffy, white clouds,
In a steaming sun.

The deep blue sea,
The long brown seaweed,
Foamy sea that floats,
Rippling down the sand.

The golden sand,
The scattered pebbles,
Weaver fish that hide,
Crabs that *bite*.

Holly Collins (9)
St Wystan's School, Repton

Sea

Beautiful sky,
Scared seagulls,
Frothy clouds,
Steaming sun.

Salty sea,
Roaring waves,
Foamy splashes,
Slimy seaweed.

Shiny rock pools,
Small shells,
Scattered pebbles,
Hot sand.

Tom Chandler (9)
St Wystan's School, Repton

The Sea

The clear blue sky
Crying seagulls,
Puffy, white clouds
Glistening sun.

Calm blue sea
Fish swimming fast,
Slimy seaweed
Floating in the salty sea.

Rough seashells
Children playing,
Tall sandcastles
Buckets and spades.

Amber Holgate (9)
St Wystan's School, Repton

The Sea

Glistening sun,
In the blue sky,
Big fluffy clouds,
Floating in mid-air.

Glittering sea,
Beautiful fish,
Roaring waves,
Crash on the seashore.

Sticky sand,
On the seashore,
Laughing children,
Having fun.

Stefan Harban (9)
St Wystan's School, Repton

Sea Seasons

Turquoise-blue sky
Drifts slowly with the white clouds,
As seagulls soar
Around the gleaming sun.

Azure-blue waves crashing
Like angels from above,
People in the rock pools
Everyone having fun.

Sandy rocks by the shore
Castles being built,
Children playing on the sand
In the roasting midday sun.

Rebecca Downs (10)
St Wystan's School, Repton

The Sea

Beautiful blue sky
Singing seagulls,
Big fluffy clouds
Golden sunshine.

Blue, salty sea
Schools of fish,
Calm sea
Slimy seaweed.

Glistening rock pools
Clipping crabs,
Hot sand
Shining shells.

Lucy Adams (9)
St Wystan's School, Repton

Underwater School

Underwater school,
Is so great,
With all the fish,
We're going to be late.

Underwater school,
Is so cool,
With a mini teacher,
Ready to rule.

Underwater school,
The bell has rang,
Running like lightning,
To see our mam.

Claire Louise Barr & Bethany Gray (9)
Thanet Primary School, Hull

Shark Jaws

All alone in the sea
Sharks all around
Sharks coming closer
No other soul to be found.

Swimming away, *splosh, splish, splash,*
Gobbles up his wallet, no more cash.
Cutting through the water, like a knife through butter,
This shark is clever, it's no nutter.

Here comes a rowing boat,
Hooray! I'm saved!
Guess who's rowing it?
It's my mate!

Connor Hadfield & Alex Foster (9)
Thanet Primary School, Hull

Fish Search

As big as a gorilla searching for food,
I wouldn't try to get it in a mood,
In the water the fishes sleep,
Then the bears would try to leap.

Water crashing and bashing down the waterfall,
Fishes making a *flip, flap, flop,*
The day is over, hooray, hooray,
Just be careful about tomorrow's day.

Kieran Poskitt (9)
Thanet Primary School, Hull

Tropical Beach

The wind blew very lightly,
The sun looked down brightly,
The sea swayed very friendly,
Swish, swish, swish,
The palm trees blew to the side very calmly,
The dolphins jumped excitedly,
The fish swam very happily,
The sky was very blue,
The golden sand for me and you,
The sea was almost as blue as the sky,
The trees were very high,
The whale made a splash,
As the dolphin made a *splosh, splash, splosh.*

Aimey Freeman, Emily Attwood & Kelly Louise Phillipson (9)
Thanet Primary School, Hull

Shark Bait

Sharks all around us,
I'm so scared,
To be eaten,
We'll be third.

They jump out and catch us,
Splish, splash, splosh,
They only got my best mate,
Oh, my gosh!

Adam Kyle (9)
Thanet Primary School, Hull

Moonlight Water

When the moonlight shines,
Under the beautiful water,
The moon is like a football reaching for goal,
It shines, sparkles, like ten million stars.

Waves lapping on the seashore,
I think they're asking for more,
I wonder if they are asking,
But we'll never know and it really makes me happy.

Connor Hemingway (9)
Thanet Primary School, Hull

Underwater Life

Ocean, ocean,
Look at the motion,
The water's all around,
With very little sound.

Whale, whale,
I like to sail,
Fish, fish,
On my dish.

James Heath & Shane Radford (9)
Thanet Primary School, Hull

Waterfall In The Jungle

The waterfall crashes down on the rocks,
The waterfall bubbles and gurgles,
The waterfall rapidly crushes the rocks,
The waterfall is swishing in the jungle.

The swishing of the waterfall makes the jungle grow,
It swirls and curls like a whirlpool,
The waterfall crashing down on the rocks, like a smashing window,
The water making the rocks fade away.

Nathan Woolhouse & Lloyd Morrison (9)
Thanet Primary School, Hull

Bayview Island

Come to Bayview Island,
Covered in golden sand,
The sea is as calm as a whale asleep,
You will not hear a single peep.

Looking out at the sea so blue,
Crisp, cool, calm, waiting for you,
Below the tree you can get some shade,
Sit and watch the sun fade.

Jordan Scott & Liam Alan Hutchinson (9)
Thanet Primary School, Hull

Tropical Island

The sea was calm
As I lay on the beach
And there, behind us, was the quality bar,
I came here in my best car,
The sun dyed my hair blonde.

The palm trees are green,
The treasure chest was hidden,
Behind the bar door,
When I was coming home, the sun turned me brown,
I played hide-and-seek beneath the bar floor.

Lauren Scarah & Amy Mail (9)
Thanet Primary School, Hull

Underwater

There's more to see,
Red fish, yellow, blue and green,
Wow! There is an octopus,
Splish, splash, plop,
How many tentacles?
One . . . two . . . three . . . four . . . five . . . six . . . seven . . .
Eight of them,
Ouch! What was that?
It's a crab,
You must be lost,
There you are, back where you belong.

Adam Hilton (9)
Thanet Primary School, Hull

Holidays

Holidays have a nice, warm pool
Holidays are so cool,
Holidays are boiling hot,
I put something to eat in my pot.

When I go home, I am sad,
So I cry on my dad,
When I get in the car, I have a nap,
When I am home, I unpack.

Katie Drury (9)
Thanet Primary School, Hull

The Water On The Island

The water was as blue as the sky
And as clean as a new T-shirt
The water is splashing and sploshing against the rocks
Water as blue as the sky
Water always is as cold as being in the freezer
Freezer was that cold, that you could turn into an ice cube
If you moved.

Chloe Warrior (9)
Thanet Primary School, Hull

The Water Bears

Bears, bears swimming in water,
Bears, bears looking for their daughters,
Bears, bears catching their food,
Bears, bears in a big, bad mood,
Bears, bears found their daughters,
Bears, bears found their food,
The bears are out of their mood,
All the bears are happy again!
Bears, bears fishing for their food,
The fish swim as fast as a speedboat,
The water was crashing and smashing
And the bears were moaning and groaning.

Abbigail Clixby & Chloe Fothergill (9)
Thanet Primary School, Hull

The Waterfall

There are a lot of living things
It's beautiful
It has leaves
The environment is great
The plants will stay alive
Because the waterfall will keep them wet
The water splashes on the rocks *smash!*

Ryan Thomas Weaver (9)
Thanet Primary School, Hull

Bears

Hunting near water falling
And the bears are calling
Cool, icy water around
With cold, wet fish in their jaws.

Lewis Taylor (9)
Thanet Primary School, Hull

The Magic Window

There once was a magic window,
Hidden away in the corner of the room . . .

A lion looked through the window
And saw himself roaming free on the green, green grass.

Adam Equinox looked through the window
And saw his loving parents.

My dad looked through the window
And saw his dad looking very happy to see him.

A monkey looked through the window
And saw himself in the world's biggest banana factory.

Voldemort looked through the window
And saw himself kill Harry Potter.

Seb Shields (9)
Warwick Junior School, Warwick

The Magic Window

There once was a magic window
Hidden away in the corner of the room . . .

Horrid Henry looked through the window
And saw Perfect Peter having to do detention
On a Saturday morning.

King Henry VIII looked through the window
And saw the axeman cutting off another traitor's head.

Steve Irwin looked through the window
And saw himself alive and swimming away from the stingray
Before it stabbed him through the heart.

Will Button looked through the window
And saw himself playing the clarinet
At the Royal Albert Hall.

Miss Beck looked through the window
And saw all the boys in her class
Writing a brilliant poem!

Martin Johnson looked through the window
And saw himself lifting the World Cup
And the crowd was screaming.

The lion looked through the window
And saw himself free
Catching the fastest gazelle on the plain.

Sam Button (9)
Warwick Junior School, Warwick

The Magic Window

There once was a magic window
Hidden away in the corner of the room . . .

Count Olaf looked through the window
And saw the Baudelaire fortune in his hands.

Guy Fawkes looked through the window
And saw himself blowing up King James.

Andrew Flintoff looked through the window
And saw himself winning The Ashes.

The lion in a zoo looked through the window
And saw himself free.

My grandma looked through the window
And saw herself sprinting down the road.

James Cusworth (9)
Warwick Junior School, Warwick

Anger

As the fire seeps through the forest
The trees are alight
The smell is woody, smoky and sticky
Sounds you hear
The roaring
The animals
The rats and wombats
The taste is hot, bitter and stiff
And it reminds you of the fires of the Outback.

Sam Martin (9)
Warwick Junior School, Warwick

The Devil

The Devil is the dark king,
He has a black diamond ring,
He is ever so smart
And amazing at art,
You will find him in an old dark well,
Then he jumps out and sends you to
Hell!

Jai Hayer (9)
Warwick Junior School, Warwick

Emotions

Anger is red
Like an elephant on rampage.

Hate is black
Like a demon's lair.

Sadness is light blue
Like a sea of tears.

Love is pink
Like a lovely rose in summer.

Happiness is light green
Like a luscious meadow in spring.

Fear is grey
Like a stormy night.

Hope is white
Like a guardian angel.

Spite is dark green
Like a muddy swamp.

Willie Priestley (9)
Warwick Junior School, Warwick

The Magic Window

There once was a magic window
Hidden away in a corner of a room . . .

Homer Simpson looked through the window
And saw the biggest Krusty Burger in the world.

Henry VII looked through the window
And saw himself sitting on the throne of England.

My sister looked through the window
And saw herself driving.

A mouse looked through the window
And saw the moon made of cheese.

Steven Gerrard looked through the window
And saw England winning the World Cup.

Michael Richards (9)
Warwick Junior School, Warwick

The Magic Window

There was once a magic window
Hidden away in the corner of the room . . .

Matilda looked through the window
She saw herself with a loving family.

Hitler looked through the window
And saw himself ruling Britain.

Chris Moyles looked through the window
And saw himself winning the X Factor.

When the monkey looked out of the window
He saw that the zoo was made of bananas.

David Beckham looked through the window
And he still played football for England.

I wonder what the window will tell me?

Laurence Johnson (9)
Warwick Junior School, Warwick

The Magic Window

There once was a magic window
Hidden away in the corner of the room . . .

Horrid Henry looked through the window
And saw himself as king ruling Perfect Peter.

Blackbeard looked through the window
And saw himself ruling the high seas.

Gordon Ramsay looked through the window
And saw himself as the best chef ever.

My sister looked through the window
And saw herself without a nut allergy.

Mr Lewis looked through the window
And saw his class all brilliant at maths.

David Beckham looked through the window
And saw himself as England captain lifting the World Cup.

A lion looked through the window
And saw itself running free in the wild.

Jamie Shillcock (9)
Warwick Junior School, Warwick

The Magic Window

There once was a magic window
Hidden away in the corner of the room . . .

Horrid Henry looked through the window
And saw himself as king.

David Beckham looked through the window
And saw himself score a goal in the World Cup final.

An elephant looked through the window
And saw himself free in the green, green grass.

A lion looked through the window
And saw himself kill a bull.

Matt Dawson looked through the window
And saw himself score a try against New Zealand.

Alexander Harper (9)
Warwick Junior School, Warwick

Anger

Anger is red like a river of blood
And the Devil's horns
It feels like the rough surface of bricks
It sounds like screaming and guns
It reminds me of death
It smells like the horrible red ooze
Dripping from a monster.

Gordon Carr (9)
Warwick Junior School, Warwick

The Magic Window

There once was a magic window
Hidden away in the corner of the room . . .

David looked through the window
And saw Johannes alive and walking with him.

Sir Francis Drake looked through the window
And saw himself beating the mighty Spanish galleons.

Jamie Oliver looked through the window
And saw people eating healthy meals.

Guy Canning looked through the window
And saw himself with his own racehorse.

Mr Lewis looked through the window
And saw no marking to do.

David Beckham looked through the window
And saw himself back in the England team.

A zebra looked through the window
And saw himself free in green fields, eating all the grass he could.

Joe Canning (9)
Warwick Junior School, Warwick

The Magic Window

There once was a window
Hidden away in the corner of the room . . .

Horrid Henry looked through the window
And saw himself as king.

The Greeks looked through the window
And saw themselves ruling the world.

Michael Morpurgo looked through the window
And saw himself as the richest author ever.

My dad looked through the window
And saw himself as a very famous engineer.

Mr Canning looked through the window
And saw Warwick School as the leading school in Britain.

Michael Schumacher looked through the window
And saw himself as the F1 World Champion.

A lion looked through the window
And saw himself roaming free.

Callum James (9)
Warwick Junior School, Warwick

Happiness

Happiness is orange, like the dawning sun
Happiness feels like you've passed an exam
Happiness sounds like a singing bird in summer
Happiness smells like steak and chips
Happiness tastes like chocolate
Happiness reminds me of my family.

Alex Simpson (9)
Warwick Junior School, Warwick

The Unlucky Day

This strange day
One very unlucky day
It was an unlucky day
Because it was Wednesday the 13th!

It was one of the most
Unluckiest days ever
Thunderstorms and lightning
Anything unlucky you can imagine.

But just then
Mum said
'We're going
to get a puppy.'

When we got there
We found just the one
Small, cute, blond-haired
Then I called him, Lucky!

When we stepped out
I felt the warm air
As the sun came out
And it was lucky again!

Ollie Shearman (9)
Warwick Junior School, Warwick

The Magic Window

There once was a magic window
Hidden away in the corner of the room . . .

Chris Moyles looked through the window
And saw himself winning the X Factor.

David Beckham looked through the window
And saw himself being captain for England again.

My brother looked through the window
And saw himself at the 2012 Olympics.

David looked through the window
And saw Johanne's face again.

Mr Frize looked through the window
And saw Australia winning The Ashes.

Will Jackson (9)
Warwick Junior School, Warwick

Anger

Anger sounds like a steam train rushing through a deserted station
Anger tastes like the blood of a devil
Anger feels like a meteor at 200 degrees
Anger looks like a red-hot pan which is incredibly hot
Anger smells like a mad, younger boy
Anger reminds me of trouble.

Alex Fox (9)
Warwick Junior School, Warwick

The Magic Window

There was once a magic window
Hidden away in the corner of the room . . .

Kensuke looked through the window
And saw his happy family laughing and playing.

Anthony looked through the window
And saw Cleopatra alive and in his arms.

Steven Gerrard looked through the window
And saw the World Cup in his arms, shining.

Michael Jackson looked through the window
And saw his nose, perfect at last.

Miss Beck looked through the window
And saw herself leading the Liverpool team out at Anfield.

I looked through the window
I closed my eyes, for this is where dreams come true.

Harnek Singh (9)
Warwick Junior School, Warwick

The Magic Mirror

There once was a magic mirror
Hidden away in the corner of the room . . .

The Baudelaire children looked into the mirror
And saw their parents alive and well.

Henry VIII looked into the mirror
And saw himself thinner.

Tony Blair looked into the mirror
And saw himself as Prime Minister until he dies.

My mum looked into the mirror
And saw herself winning the lottery.

Mr Elston looked into the mirror
And saw the whole school lining up quietly.

Thierry Henry looked into the mirror
And saw himself lifting the UEFA Champions League cup.

I looked into the mirror
And saw myself as captain of England football team.

Louis Hawking (9)
Warwick Junior School, Warwick

The Magic Window

There once was a magic window
Hidden away in the corner of the room . . .

Streaker looked through the window
And saw himself running at 100mph.

Tutankhamun looked through the window
And saw himself ruling the world.

Tony Blair looked through the window
And saw himself as Prime Minister forever.

My dog looked through the window
And saw meat in a huge bowl.

Mr Elston looked through the window
And saw nobody get an order mark.

Beckham looked through the window
And saw England winning the World Cup.

A lion looked through the window
And saw it was raining steaks.

Henry McGovern (9)
Warwick Junior School, Warwick

Happiness

Happiness sounds like trickling water in the brook
Happiness feels like a puppy's soft, warm fur
Happiness smells like oozing, melted chocolate on a fountain
Happiness looks like blossoming roses in springtime
Happiness tastes like doughnuts with jam coming out
Happiness reminds me of good times when I was small.

Toby Ashworth (9)
Warwick Junior School, Warwick

Santa Claus

Snow falls in winter
It's really quite fun
For that's when Santa comes
And that's all the fun

He comes on December 24th
In the middle of the night
When Santa's on your roof
As quick as a flash
He's in and out delivering presents

He flies like the wind
As he soars through the sky
With Rudolph as his light
He can see anything he likes.

George Burbidge (9)
Warwick Junior School, Warwick

Why Bovver?

Why bovver?

Whenever you're late for school, the traffic's bad
When you decide to walk, the weather's bad.

In chemistry, whenever you know how to do it
Your partner blows up the lab (you take the blame)
When you don't know how to do it
Neither does your partner.

In plays, when you rehearse, you know the words
In the performance, you forget the words.

When you're chewing gum in class the teacher tells you off
Then, behind the teacher's back, the class bully starts his patrol
(Guess who gets away with it?)

Whenever there's something good for lunch
The second choice is equally good.
Whenever there's something bad for lunch
The second choice is equally bad.

And when my mum collects me
And I say, 'Nice top, Mum!'
She's says, 'What's wrong with my shoes?'

Why do I bovver?

Tobias Sims (9)
Warwick Junior School, Warwick

Do You Believe In Father Christmas?

'Do you believe in Father Christmas?'
Asked my father on a cold winter's night.
'No, I don't,' said I, 'why?'
'Because he's coming tonight,
What would you like?'
'I don't know
I've got to go to bed now,' said I.
I woke up in the dead of night
And looked out of my window.
Everything was white and still
So it had obviously been snowing.
Suddenly, I heard a noise and turned around
There was nothing there
So I looked in the cupboard
There he was, all plump and jolly!
Father Christmas! In red and white clothes!
Then he vanished and appeared at the other end of the room
He hung up my stocking and disappeared!

Sam Hillcox (9)
Warwick Junior School, Warwick

The Magic Window

There once was a magic window
Hidden in the corner of the room . . .

Harry Potter looked through the window
And saw his parents alive and well.

Edward the Conqueror looked through the window
And saw himself as king forever.

Billie Piper looked through the window
And saw herself winning an Oscar.

My dad looked through the window
And saw himself as Prime Minister.

Mr Lewis looked through the window
And saw the whole class getting into university.

David Beckham looked through the window
And saw himself winning the World Cup.

A lion looked through the window
And saw a year's supply of food.

I looked through the window
And saw myself with the rest of the Arsenal team, holding the FA Cup.

Bhavan Thiara (9)
Warwick Junior School, Warwick

Anger

Anger is red like a bursting balloon
It feels like water as hot as lava
It sounds like a kettle about to explode
It smells like a shower full of steam
It tastes like soup as hot as fire
It looks like your dad about to go mad
It reminds me of the *big bang!*

James Cleary (9)
Warwick Junior School, Warwick

The Magic Window

There once was a magic window
Hidden away in the corner of the room . . .

Horrid Henry looked through the window
And saw he was a king.

Mr Frize looked through the window
And saw Australia winning The Ashes.

The penguin looked through the window
And saw the world was full of fish.

I looked through the window
And saw myself becoming a footballer.

King Richard III looked through the window
And saw himself killing Henry Tudor and becoming king.

My dad looked through the window
And saw himself as a billionaire.

Jonny Wilkinson looked through the window
And saw himself playing for England again and winning the World Cup.

Wayne Rooney looked through the window
And saw Manchester United winning the Champions League
And the FA Premier League.

Freddie Ashworth (9)
Warwick Junior School, Warwick

The Magic Window

There once was a magic window
Hidden away in the corner of the room . . .

I looked through the window
And saw myself winning the FA Cup with Liverpool.

A penguin looked through the window
And saw itself eating fresh fish in the Antarctic.

Miss Beck looked through the window
And saw everyone in the school working hard.

Tony Blair looked through the window
And saw himself being Prime Minister forever.

Richard III looked through the window
And saw himself being crowned King of England.

Andy Murray looked through the window
And saw himself winning Wimbledon.

Hiccup Horrendous Haddock looked through the window
And saw himself as a Viking hero.

My dad looked through the window
And saw himself as the best actor ever.

Sam Woodyatt (9)
Warwick Junior School, Warwick

Unlucky Ben

There once was a boy called Ben
He went fishing, but it started spitting
Then he went sailing, but it started raining
Then he went running, but it started hailing
Then he went abseiling, but it started thundering
Then he went to climbing, but he got struck by lightning
No more Ben!

Ben Taylor (9)
Warwick Junior School, Warwick

The Magic Window

There once was a magic window
Hidden away in the corner of the room . . .

A lion looked through the window
And saw himself free in the wild.

An Athenean soldier looked through the window
And saw that Athens ruled Greece.

Mr Lewis looked through the window
And saw all of his class becoming prefects.

Henry Ford looked through the window
And saw that he had sold Jaguar and kept Land Rover.

Mrs Twit looked through the window
And saw herself dumping Mr Twit.

Richard Phillips (9)
Warwick Junior School, Warwick

The Magic Window

There once was a magic window
Hidden away in the corner of the room . . .

Horrid Henry looked through the window
And saw himself as king.

Adolf Hitler looked through the window
And saw himself ruling the whole world.

David Beckham looked through the window
And saw himself playing for England again.

My brother and I looked through the window
And saw ourselves playing for Liverpool.

Tim Henman looked through the window
And saw himself winning the tennis league all the time.

A sheep looked through the window
And saw himself in the field, eating lots of grass.

Hamish Kerr (9)
Warwick Junior School, Warwick

Anger Is . . .

Anger is red like an erupting, fierce volcano
Anger tastes like red-hot chilli peppers
Anger sounds like an over-heated kettle boiling
Anger feels as hot as sunburn, scalding my hand
Anger looks like a fried tomato
Anger smells like the sweat of a professional athlete
Anger reminds me of my sisters when I go into their room.

Matthew Riley (9)
Warwick Junior School, Warwick

Feelings

Anger is red like blood dripping from a dead man
Hate is black like a dark cloud floating over the universe
Sadness is aqua like tears falling into the sea
Happiness is white like a seagull flying happily
Fear is purple like a scared man in a scary moment.

Tohmev Singh (9)
Warwick Junior School, Warwick

Golf

Golf is a funny game,
Sometimes you've got it,
Sometimes you've lost it,
Sometimes satisfied,
Sometimes angry,
Golf is a funny game.

Golf is a funny game,
Sometimes too wet,
Sometimes too dry,
Sometimes too dark,
Sometimes too light,
Golf is a funny game.

Harry Fitzpatrick (9)
Warwick Junior School, Warwick

To A Dear Friend, Todd

Here lies our dear friend, Todd
What a shame!
What happened, we can't tell
We don't know, but what was left
I thought was theft
That greedy old shark
What a shame, oh please, oh God
Poor, poor Todd.

Todd Freeman (10)
Warwick Junior School, Warwick